SOARING HAWK!
A young Tony catches major air on a ramp in San Diego, California.

ROBERT BECK

tony hawk
CHAIRMAN OF THE BOARD

SCHOLASTIC INC.
New York Toronto London Auckland Sydney
Mexico City New Delhi Hong Kong Buenos Aires

contents

PHOTO MOSAIC BY RICH FRISH

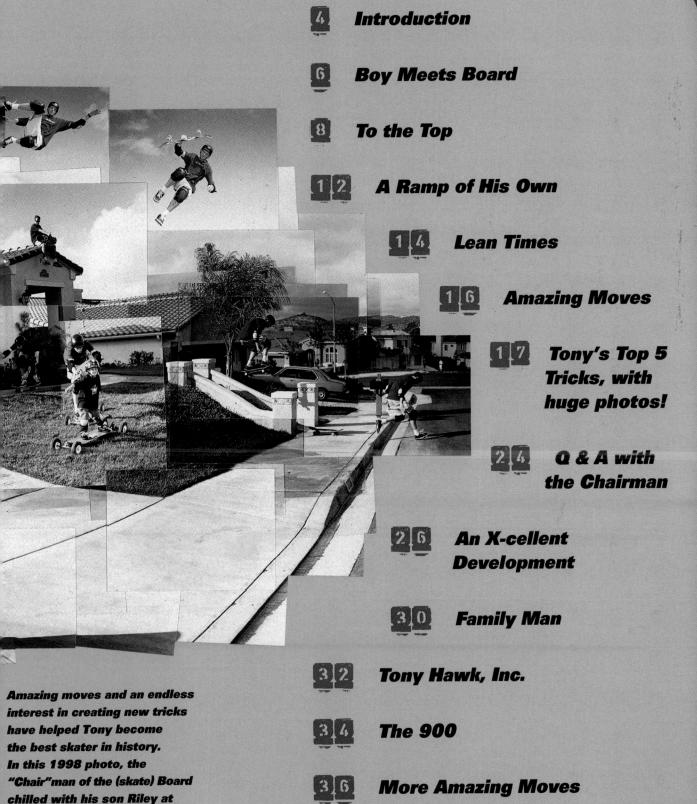

Amazing moves and an endless interest in creating new tricks have helped Tony become the best skater in history. In this 1998 photo, the "Chair"man of the (skate) Board chilled with his son Riley at their Carlsbad, California, home. But Tony doesn't hang around doing nothing very often!

tony hawk

MIKI VUCKOVICH

"Now it's just so fun to know that there's a skate park in almost every city and a scene everywhere you go."
— Tony Hawk

Skateboarding – and Tony – has come a long way. In 1983, he (above, right, at the Upland Pipeline) was a new pro in an odd sport. By 2000 (left), he was the legendary superstar of the spectacle called extreme sports.

Tony Hawk had no idea when he first stepped onto a skateboard, in 1977, that he would change the way the world looked at the activity, or that he would eventually make a lot of money doing something he loved. Back then, Tony had bigger problems — like figuring out how to turn without running into the fence that bordered the alley behind his house.

That took a day to learn, but Tony did get the hang of it. From then on, he didn't stop learning, and when he had learned everything other skaters were doing, he began inventing his own tricks. Two decades later, he has created more than 80 tricks and landed the 900 — what many people consider the hardest trick in skateboarding history.

What's left for Tony Hawk to accomplish in skateboarding? He has won more than 70 contests, way more than any other skater. He has started his own skateboard company, called Birdhouse Projects; written a best-selling autobiography *(Hawk: Occupation: Skateboarder)*, and helped create one of the most popular video games in the world *(Tony Hawk's Pro Skater)*. He also has his own shoe and clothing companies. He has a great family, a dog, and a skateboard — what else could he possibly need?

But Tony continues to push himself. He invents tricks and builds custom ramps so that he can practice tricks he can't do anywhere else. At 30-plus, he has just as much determination as the 9-year-old kid who dedicated his whole day to learning how to turn his first board in an alley behind his house.

That's why Tony Hawk is Chairman of the Board! ◆

Boy Mee

When Tony was 9 years old, his brother, Steve, changed his life. Steve was 12 years older than Tony, and he loved surfing. The Hawks lived in San Diego, California, not far from the Pacific Ocean. Most mornings, Steve woke up early to surf before going to school.

Because Steve loved surfing, he had tried out "sidewalk surfing." That's what early skateboarding was called. At first, skateboarders were surfers who skated when the waves were flat. They pretended to be riding a wave while they skated down the street.

Steve had an old banana board in the garage. He had forgotten about it until he was playing with Tony one day in 1977. He took Tony to a nearby alley, showed him how to balance on the board, and gave him a push. Tony rolled and rolled until he ran into a fence. He couldn't figure out how to turn! Steve spent the rest of the day teaching him how to avoid smashing into things.

Falling in love It was not love at first sight. Tony thought of the board as just another toy, like a Nerf football. Tony also played baseball and basketball. Slowly, over the next year, though, he began skating more and more.

One weekend, the mother of one of Tony's friends took the neighborhood kids to a skate park, in San Diego, called Oasis. Skaters whipped around riding the bowls, banks, pools, and other obstacles of the park. Tony said the skaters whipping around Oasis were like molecules in a nuclear reaction. He loved it.

After that, Tony wanted to go every weekend. He nagged his parents to drive him there. If his brother or sisters were visiting, he made *them* take him. Soon he was asking for rides after school. He wanted to go every *day*. At school, he doodled pictures of skaters and did all of his class projects on skateboarding. Tony had become a skateboard addict! ◆

When Tony was 9, his big brother, Steve, gave him an old banana board and said "You should try this." Soon, Tony was catching air (above) and begging rides to a nearby skate park.

Non-stop skating turned Tony into a tiger on the ramp. Inverts, aerials, finger flips, and more were part of his skating vocab. By the time the National Skateboard Association was founded, in 1983, Tony had turned pro, developed his own style, and created some awesome tricks.

J. GRANT BRITTAIN

To The TOP

At age 12, Tony became the youngest member of Powell and Peralta's Bones Brigade, thanks to Stacy (with camera). Suddenly, the skinny, little kid was competing against skaters five years older, and teaming up with his heroes! A few years later, he began appearing in Stacy's cool skate videos.

Tony had such a bad temper as a child that he often refers to himself as a "demon boy." Skateboarding changed that. "He wasn't as competitive with other people anymore," said Steve.

Instead, Tony was competitive with himself. That's what he liked about skateboarding: It wasn't a team sport. He didn't like letting his team down. With skateboarding, Tony could only let *himself* down — and he wasn't about to do that. That's why he would practice a single trick all day long.

First Contest   Tony was 11 when he competed in his first skateboard contest. There were more than 100 skaters in his age group! Tony was so nervous before the contest that he developed a stomachache. He didn't skate well and fell on easy tricks.

Tony had let himself down, and that was the worst feeling he had ever had. So, after that, Tony got serious about contests. He would skate the park before each competition. He drew a diagram of the pool (competitions were often held in swimming pools). Then he would map out where he would do his tricks and memorize his planned run.

Tony's strategy worked! He did a lot better. By the end of the year, he had won his age class. He also had become a member of the Oasis Skatepark team.

At 11, Tony also got his first sponsor, Dogtown Skateboards. Dogtown went out of business soon, but Tony quickly found another sponsor: Stacy Peralta, who owned part of Powell and Peralta, the hottest skateboard company at the time. Stacy named the Powell group of skaters The Bones Brigade.

Teenage Pro   Tony's first big, out-of-town contest for Powell was in Jacksonville, Florida. He fell during his run and was so upset that he refused to talk to anybody afterward. But Stacy was a great coach, and with his help and hours of practice, Tony improved even more quickly than before.

Before one local skating contest, in 1982, Stacy turned to Tony and asked him if he wanted to turn pro. Tony shrugged and said yes. He skated well

CONTINUED ON PAGE 10 >>>

To The TOP

A year after he turned pro, Tony began to win almost every contest he entered. And he won all over the country. In 1986, he and Lester Kasai (below) skated at a big event in Virginia Beach, Virginia. You can guess from Tony's look that he did not win!

and placed third against the best skaters in the world! He was 14.

Circus Skater Despite his early skateboarding success, Tony had a problem. He was too skinny to do some of the harder aerial tricks. He needed more weight to generate enough momentum to fly above the ramp. But no matter how much food he ate, Tony couldn't put on weight.

So he invented a different way to catch air. Instead of grabbing his board early, like all the other skaters, he ollied (did a no-handed aerial) into the air and then grabbed his board. That way he could use his legs more to launch himself off the lip of the ramp and do more tricks. The new style worked, but it looked a lot different from anybody else's style. Other pros made fun of Tony's skating. Some called him a "cheater" because of his technique.

Tony also invented a lot of tricks in which he would flip his board and then put it back under his feet.

ROBERT BECK

Today, every skater does flip tricks, but back then, skaters called him a "circus skater" for doing them.

By 1985, Oasis had closed down. Skateboarding had become less popular. But Tony kept skating with his friends, at Del Mar Skatepark, in San Diego. He kept inventing tricks, innovative tricks. In a few years, all the skaters who had made fun of Tony were trying to learn from him!

J. GRANT BRITTAIN

Champion of the World After Tony turned pro, it took him awhile to get used to skating against older, more experienced skaters. He bobbed all over the contest results. Sometimes he would win, and sometimes he'd place 10th. When Tony skated poorly, it upset him, and he practiced harder. Soon he began winning a lot. He became the first pro skater to win three vert contests in a row.

In 1983, the National Skateboard Association was founded. It governed the world skateboard rankings. Tony was declared world champion. He was 15. ◆

In the mid-1980's, Tony invented many tricks no one else dreamed of – such as Airwalk, Madonna, and Stalefish – and some tricks that no one else could do. The 720 was so surprising that it landed Tony in a Ripley's Believe It or Not comic.

A Ramp
OF HIS OWN

Tony and his dad, Frank (left), designed an array of ramps for the house in Fallbrook. The backyard bowl (below) was a dream come true.

When Tony first turned pro, he didn't get rich quick. He had a school friend design his first board graphic, of a hawk swooping down for the kill, and he sent it to Stacy Peralta. Stacy used it to design a Tony Hawk board, even though Tony had meant it to be just a vague idea of what he wanted. The board came out and sold horribly. The first monthly royalty check Tony received came to 85 cents! In the whole world, one person had bought his board.

Stacy and Tony quickly worked on a new graphic, with some help from Powell's designer. It was a hawk skull, and everybody loved it. Tony started selling more boards.

By the time he was 17, Tony had sold thousands of boards. He was earning about $70,000 a year! Tony had so much money that he decided to buy his own house, in Carlsbad, California, near his parents' home. He was a senior in high school.

Backyard Bowl In 1988, Tony moved into another house, in Fallbrook, California, away from the city of San Diego. He bought it so that he would have room to build a private ramp in his backyard. Tony spent $30,000 building a 12-foot-high vert ramp attached to a wooden bowl. He also built a seven-foot-high mini-ramp outside his back door. He could wake up, open his door, and skate without setting foot on his lawn!

Tony won all the N.S.A. world titles from 1983 through 1994. The only thing that stopped him from winning world championships was the N.S.A.'s going out of business in the early 1990's.

Being the Best Tony says the reason he kept winning was that he *always* thought his skating could improve. If he won a contest but didn't skate up to his expectations, he would be upset, go home, and work harder. During most contests Tony would unleash a trick nobody had seen before.

"The best thing is skating at home with a few friends and trying new stuff," Tony told S.I. For Kids. "I don't like competition that much." He "retired" for a while and enjoyed his backyard skate park.

But being the best in the world put a lot of pressure on Tony. People's expectations of him became too high. They expected him to win every time. If he didn't win, skaters made a huge deal out of it because it didn't happen that often. The pressure became too much for Tony. When he was 19 years old, he decided to stop competing.

But Tony's retirement from competition didn't last long. After a few months, he developed a new attitude. He returned determined to skate just for fun from then on.

Tony was so good that he still won almost every contest. ◆

Lean Times

Skateboarding's popularity dropped in the early 1990's, and, suddenly, Tony didn't have it so easy. He went from making about $20,000 a month to making about that much in a *year*. Skating fans were rare. One time, he went to give a skating demonstration and only 25 people showed up. A few years earlier, more than 5,000 people would have shown up.

None of that affected Tony's love for skating. He still skated every day. But he didn't have money to fix his ramp, and it began to deteriorate. He had to dodge holes in the wood as he skated, and he often didn't have anybody to skate with. He would just plug in a portable stereo and skate by himself.

In the early 1990's, Tony kept busy editing and performing in videos. Here he is, in 1993, on the set of a 3-D music video directed by Aaron Chang.

A Reel Job This went on for about five years, so Tony had to change his lifestyle to make ends meet. He sold the house with the private ramp and moved into a smaller home. He bought a cheaper car. Tony borrowed $8,000 from his parents to buy editing equipment and began editing videos for skateboard companies. He helped surfer Brad Gerlach make instructional surfing videos. During this time, he also starred in his own skate video, *The End*.

Skaters looked a little different in 1990. Now, the pads are beefier, the shoes better, and haircuts don't require as much bleach!

RICHARD MACKSON

Bird Man In 1991, Tony decided he wanted complete control of his skateboarding future. So, he partnered with an old skating friend to start Birdhouse Projects. He put all of his extra money into the company. If it failed, Tony would be in a worse financial position than he had ever been. But, if it succeeded, he would be in a better position than ever. It was a gamble, but Tony thought of it the same way as learning a new trick — he'd do everything he could to make it happen. One of the ways to do that was go on tour.

Ever since Tony had graduated from high school, in 1986, he spent summers on the road. Summer is the busiest time of the year for pro skaters because the weather is warm and kids are out of school. Tony traveled around the country — and around the world — competing and giving demonstrations. The lean times of the early '90s didn't stop the summer travels, it just thinned the crowds out a bit. ◆

J. GRANT BRITTAIN

AMAZING MOVES

Tony's career has been like a human highlight film of awesome tricks. Check out some of his amazing moves.

1 >>

2 >>

<< **3**

<< **4**

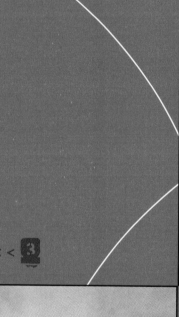

5 >>

In the mid-1990's, flip tricks became popular, leading to a new type of skating. No problem. Tony adapted with innovative flips like this heel-flip varial lien air.

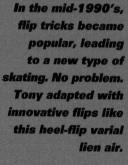

6 >>

AMAZING MOVES

Skateboard tricks have some strange names. Here's Tony doing a frontside hurricane on his backyard ramp in 1990.

23

Q&A
with tony

MIKI VUKOVICK

Tony's Favorite Stuff

13 Questions

COURTESY OF TONY HAWK

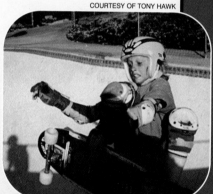

At first, catching air was scary for Tony.

1 What did it feel like the first time you caught air?

It was scary because I wasn't sure how to land properly. I worked my way up the wall. When I got to the top of the pool, I was more scared to fall than I was to land the trick because I was so high up. So I landed it.

2 Who would you most like to meet?

Wile E. Coyote, super genius. I liked his persistence in the face of constant adversity, no matter what happened. [Wile E. Coyote is a character in the *Road Runner* cartoon series.]

3 What place would you most like to visit?

Indonesia, to go surfing with my friends, who aren't the best surfers and are as afraid of huge waves as I am. That way I won't have to ride the gnarliest waves.

4 What's your most embarrassing moment?

It happened on tour in 2000. Right as our demonstration began, I dropped into a very small ramp and fell straight to the floor. There was a big hole in the ramp that I didn't see as I went down. All of my fellow pros laughed hysterically.

FIVE FAVORITE MOVIES: *Fast Times at Ridgemont High, Weird Science, Aliens, Happy Gilmore, The Sixth Sense*

FIVE FOODS: Indian, sushi, Thai, pizza, Twizzlers

FIVE CDs: Moby - *Play*; De La Soul - *Art Official Intelligence*; The Clash - *London Calling*; Jane's Addiction - *Nothing's Shocking*; Madonna - *The Immaculate Collection*

FIVE BOOKS: *Green Eggs and Ham*, by Dr. Seuss; *High Fidelity*, by Nick Hornby; Harry Potter Series, by J.K. Rowling; *The Stinky Cheese Man*, by Jon Scieszka; *Holidays in Hell*, by P.J. O'Rourke

5 What was your greatest sports thrill?

Finally landing a 900 after five years of failed attempts, in the 1999 X-Games.

6 What other sports besides skating do you dig?

Surfing and snowboarding. I surfed before I skated. My brother, Steve, would sometimes take me surfing on the weekends,

About Tony

NAME: Anthony Frank Hawk

NICKNAME: Tony

HEIGHT: 6' 3"

WEIGHT: 170 pounds

BORN: May 12, 1968, in San Diego, California

HOMETOWN: Carlsbad, California

WEBSITES: http://www.clubtonyhawk.com;
http://www.b-house.com;
http://www.hawkclothing.com;
http://www.hawkshoes.com

♦ Won 12 skateboarding world championships, from 1983 through 1994

♦ Invented more than 80 tricks, including such standards as airwalk, Madonna, frontside hurricane, 720

♦ Won 4 gold medals, 2 silvers, and 2 bronzes at the Summer X Games, from 1995 through 1999

♦ Was the baby of his family — and how! When Tony was born, his brother, Steve, was 12 years old; his sister Patricia was 18; and his sister Lenore was 21. His parents said Tony was one of the happiest surprises of their lives.

---

and sometimes I'd take the bus down to the beach by myself.

7 As a kid, who did you most admire?
Evel Knievel, a motorcycle daredevil who once jumped over 19 cars on his bike.

8 What do you wish you could do better?
Play golf. It seems fun, but I never hit the ball straight.

9 What are you really bad at?
Relaxing. I always feel like I should be doing something. I feel like I'm letting responsibilities pile up on each other when I sit still.

10 What is your secret talent?
I speak decent French. I took two years of French in school, but after visiting France at least 20 times for skateboarding events, I can understand it a lot better than I can speak it.

11 Did you ever play an instrument?
Yes, I played the violin for a few years before I started skating.

12 If you weren't skateboarding, what do you think you would be doing?
I'd be working with computers — editing video and/or doing website work.

13 What advice would you give young skaters?
Learn the basics and try not to get too frustrated. This stuff takes a long time to learn.

Watch out below! Tony does an inverted handplant on the Death Ledge at Magdalena Ecke YMCA, in Encinitas, California.

J. GRANT BRITTAIN

1 9 9 5 1 9 9 9

An X-cellent

J. GRANT BRITTAIN

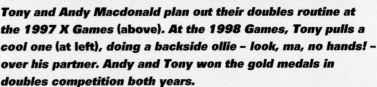

TONY DONALDSON/TDPHOTO.COM (2)

Tony and Andy Macdonald plan out their doubles routine at the 1997 X Games (above). At the 1998 Games, Tony pulls a cool one (at left), doing a backside ollie – look, ma, no hands! – over his partner. Andy and Tony won the gold medals in doubles competition both years.

Development

The X Games put "extreme" sports like skateboarding on the map and made Tony famous. At the very first X Games, in 1995, Tony pulled this method air. No wonder the fans went wild!

The X Games — or as they were called at first, the Extreme Games — premiered on ESPN in 1995. Skateboarding had begun to regain its popularity. But the X Games hurried the process along, *big time*. The X Games put the sport of skateboarding into the living rooms of millions of people around the world. Many of those people were excited by what they saw.

At the first Games, Tony won the vert contest, held in Newport, Rhode Island. He placed second in the street competition. But one of his favorite parts of those X Games was the time he looked in the TV camera during the contest and mouthed "Hi, Dad!" Tony knew his father would be at home watching. Mr. Hawk was dying of lung cancer, and it meant a lot for him to see his son getting respect from the world outside of skateboarding.

On a Roll   Each year, the X Games — and skating — grew more popular. Soon skating was more popular than it had ever been. And Tony was more famous than *he* had ever been, because he was the star of the Games.

In 1997, the X Games were held in San Diego, California. The skating

CONTINUED ON PAGE 28 > > >

An X-cellent Development

TONY DONALDSON/ICON

contest was close. Tony or any of a number of other skaters were capable of winning, but it wouldn't be easy because of the tough competition. No one watching the competition knew who would end up on top — until Tony's second run.

Best Run Ever On that run, Tony pulled out all the stops and did a lot of his best tricks. He even did tricks that he usually sketched on (that he had not perfected yet). Only this time, he landed everything. He nailed four 540s in a row! In a 540, Tony spins $1\frac{1}{2}$ times in the air while standing on his board. The announcer called it the best skateboard run ever, and Tony won the gold medal by 4.75 points.

Tony was happy with his run at the 1997 X Games, but he does *not* think it was the best run he has ever had. He thinks he had his absolute best run in a contest in Germany in 1999. At that contest, Tony landed *all* of his hardest tricks. He knew that he couldn't do a better run after that, so when it was his turn again, instead of doing his latest tricks, he only did tricks from the 1980's. All the skaters freaked out and cheered when they realized what he was doing.

Saw You on TV The X Games changed Tony's life. "Now, when I tell people I'm a professional skateboarder, they don't say, 'There's no such thing,'" he told *Time* magazine, in 1998. "Instead, they say, 'Oh, are you in the X Games?'"

Left: Tony is about to land a half-Caballerial at the 1999 X Games in San Francisco. Steve Caballero, one of Tony's heroes, invented the trick, which is a no-handed 180 air.

During the 1980's and for most of the 1990's, the only people who recognized Tony were other skaters. After a couple of X Games, people who have never stepped on a skateboard knew who Tony Hawk was and asked for his autograph.

After Tony landed the first 900 at the 1999 X Games, he had to have a security patrol escort him around the site because fans mobbed him and his family. He wouldn't have been able to move if he were walking around on his own.

The demands from reporters and newscasters were astounding too. So many newspapers and TV shows wanted to interview Tony that he had to schedule interviews around his practice runs! ◆

Above: Skateboarding just feels great! Here's a happy lien air from Tony terrific.

Family

JASON WISE/DUOMO

*Riley (above, on skateboard) **inherited his dad's love of skating and of performing for the camera – even Dad's videos.** Spencer (above, with Tony and mom Erin) **is still a little young for the sport.***

In 1990, Tony married Cindy Dunbar, his long-time girlfriend. They had a son, Riley, in 1992. After a few years, Cindy and Tony realized that married life wasn't working for them and divorced. But they remained friends and shared equally in Riley's life.

By the time Riley was 4 years old, he too had fallen in love with skateboarding. He went on tour with his dad at the age of 6 — not just to watch Tony. He skated in front of all the people who came to see Tony. Riley traveled all over the country and visited Australia, Japan, and Europe. He appeared in skating

videos and starred in a commercial for the movie *Tarzan* with his dad. People were asking for Riley's autograph before he even turned 10!

Tony says his parents' encouragement was one of the main reasons he became such a good skater. They drove him to skate parks to practice and helped organize contests around the world. Mr. Hawk helped Tony build ramps. Mr. Hawk's death, in 1995, began one of the most difficult times in Tony's life. But there was one good thing that came from that sad event: It helped Tony appreciate the effect his parents had on

him. That made him want to be as good a father to his kids as his dad had been to him.

After Tony and Cindy were divorced, Tony met Erin Lee. Erin and Tony married in 1996 and had a son, Spencer, in 1999. They live in Carlsbad, California. When he can, Tony takes the entire family with him to demos or on tours. Spencer was there when his dad landed his first 900.

If there is any one thing that Tony loves more than skateboarding, it is being a family man. ◆

Tony

RICH FRISHMAN

Tony, the skating genius, is also one amazing businessman. His companies include Birdhouse Projects, Hawk Clothing, Hawk Shoes, and 900 Films. His video games are hot too.

SCORE 567
SPECIAL

TONY HAWK'S PRO SKATER 2
Dreamcast

360 ROASTBEEF
1500

Hawk, Inc.

Skating has paid off for Tony. It seems silly to think he once thought he would never make enough money from skateboarding to support himself, much less a wife and two children. But he did. When Tony began skating, it was considered a fad. The only people who knew anything about professional skateboarding were skaters. Even as late as the early 1990's, it was a struggling sport. By the year 2000, though, *everybody* knew about skateboarding, and Tony had become the most famous skater on the planet.

Tony had also become a successful businessman, thanks to skateboarding. He co-owned Birdhouse Projects, one of the most popular skateboard companies in the world. He helped run a shoe company, called Hawk Shoes, and a clothing company, called Hawk Clothing, which makes stylish skate gear for kids.

Movies, books, and video games were all part of Tony's business. He made skateboard videos and movies, and was part-owner of a movie production house called 900 Films. Plus, he had two hugely successful video games. The first, *Tony Hawk Pro Skater*, sold over 2 million copies in 1999. *Pro Skater 2* was released in September 2000 and quickly became a best-seller as well. In August 2000, Tony's autobiography, *HAWK: Occupation: Skateboarder*, hit the bookstores. Soon *it* was on the *New York Times* extended best-seller list. On top of all that, Tony founded the Tony Hawk Foundation with his sister, Patricia, and had an internet fan club (Clubtonyhawk.com). ◆

Tony's Hawk Clothing is popular with kids. The photo above is from an advertisement Tony made with some lucky kids.

Birdhouse bearings and decks

Tony's 1998 movie

THE END

The 900

ony always had a long list of tricks that he wanted to do before he retired from skateboarding. One by one, he mastered the tricks and checked them off his list. The last trick was the 900 (which he calls, simply, "the 9".) It wasn't going to be easy to check off. The 9 was harder than any of the other tricks he had ever tried — and those tricks weren't easy! In the 900, the skater launches off the the ramp, does $2\frac{1}{2}$ rotations in the air, and lands back on the ramp. Sounds simpler than it is!

For 13 years, Tony attempted to land the trick. Missing it was *not* fun. Tony compared slamming on the 900 to being in a car wreck. It hurt his back and neck, and cut his hip. Most times, missing meant crashing from 10 feet in the air to the bottom of the halfpipe, and his knees would swell up from the impact.

Because the 900 caused so much pain when Tony fell

SHAZAMM/ESPN (3)

trying to land it, he had to space his 900 attempts far apart. He tried his first one in 1986 on a ramp in France. One time, he slammed so hard that his back went into spasms and he could barely walk. On another missed attempt, he had to visit the chiropractor *twice* in one day.

Tony came close in 1996. He landed the trick but immediately fell and fractured a rib. He planned to do the 900 for his skating video, *The End*, in 1998, but each time he got in the air, he got scared and bailed on it. He just kept remembering how much it had hurt when he fractured his rib.

Then came the best-trick contest at the 1999 X Games. Tony didn't expect to try the 900 there. But he landed another difficult trick, a varial 720 (two mid-air spins during which he spins his board 180 degrees). He said he had nothing else to do, so he decided to spin a few 9's and see how they felt. They felt the best ever.

On his 11th attempt, Tony landed the trick he had been after for so long! He surprised even himself. He didn't believe he had landed it until he was riding up the other side of the ramp. He said landing the 900 was the biggest hurdle he has gone over in his life. ◆

The date: June 27, 1999. The place: San Francisco, California. The moment: historic. Skating in the X Games, Tony landed the 900, a trick he had been trying to land for 13 years. It was the first 900 ever. Afterward, Tony said, "This is the best day of my life. This is what it all comes down to. I feel like everything had led up to now . . . The 900 was my goal."

AMAZING MOVES

The 900 is skating's ultimate trick (so far). Others have tried it, but only Tony has landed it.

1 > >

2

4 < <

7 > >

8

3 >>

5

<< 6

After the 1999 X Games, Tony landed the 900 several more times. This one, at the Mission Valley (California) YMCA, was gnarlier than the first one he did because if Tony doesn't clear the channel, he will slam. Ouch!

9 >>

AMAZING MOVES

Forever young? "I don't think
about my age when I skate.
I feel young," Tony once said.
But can the Chairman keep
pulling tricks like this
heel-flip frontside air forever?